D1523902

Euchoetry

POEMS IN THE PRESENCE
VOLUME 1

An Eric Robinson Collection

Publication Date:
March 25, 2023. Feast of the Annunciation
In Honor of the Blessed Virgin Mary in whom the
Word was made flesh in the Tabernacle of her Body

Nihil Obstat: Anthony Lilles, S.T.D.
          Censor Liborum

Imprimatur: +Most Reverend Samuel J. Aquila, S.T.L.
          Archbishop of Denver
          Denver, Colorado, USA
          August 30, 2022

Editorial Review by Jane Scharl
Internal Layout Design by Bence Szasz
Cover Design by Rocio Ortiz

Dedicated to those who have spent countless hours adoring Jesus Christ in the Blessed Sacrament.

May your faith and devotion spread like wildfire throughout the whole world.

Contents

POEMS IN THE PRESENCE
VOLUME 1

Author's Note

Where did this book come from and how should it be read?

In November 2019, after a couple months of consistently spending time with our Lord Jesus Christ in Eucharistic Adoration, I was given a simple inspiration to write a poem about the Eucharist.

This inspiration led to an idea...

What if people from all over the world were inspired to write poems about the Presence of God in the Eucharist while actually being in the Presence of God through Eucharistic Adoration?

That idea led to another...

What if those who have yet to receive our Lord in the Eucharist were so stunned by the beauty and love expressed in these poems that they were drawn into full communion with the Catholic Church and were then able to partake of the same Body, Blood, Soul, and Divinity of our Lord Jesus Christ?

If brought to fruition, these ideas could change everything. Those involved would be transfigured by the Presence of God and the world around them would be transformed!

After I spent a year of writing poems and being eager to invite others to join the movement, euchoetry.com was launched on January 1st, 2021, the feast of Mary, Mother of God. This book is just one step toward a long-term vision described in the back of the book.

I invite you to go to Eucharistic Adoration at a Catholic Church near you. Take this book with you and read one or two poems. Let them inspire you to write your own poem. More importantly, let them fill you with awe and wonder at the reality of God's Presence in your midst. Let these poems magnify your worship of Jesus Christ. This is the purpose of the book and the recommended way of reading it!

†

Silent Presence

ord,
Your silent Presence beckons all to kneel
    before your throne,
When I see your face in the Host my heart begins to groan.
No mere symbol, not even just a sign,
The Eucharist I see is altogether Divine.
You, O my Jesus, encircled by gold,
Ignite my faith to be fire-tried and bold.
Veil torn, intimacy with God is here,
Under the veiled appearance of my Savior dear.
Earth cannot fathom so great a mystery,
That you, O God, would share in our humanity.
You are Bread broken for us,
You are our Life, the sweetness that we trust.
Alas, for those I know,
Who miss your hidden Presence below.
I ask, I beg, that you open their eyes,
That they may see through the devil's lies.
May they miss you no longer as they come
    into your Church,
Built upon the Rock of Peter and spread
    throughout the Earth.

O sublime reality, Heaven and Earth are touching,
At every Mass you come to us, arms outstretching.
Here in adoration the stillness of that moment,
When the priest holds up the Host and grace comes
    in a torrent.
Sheer grace you give, sheer grace is ours,
When faith awakens to see you as you are.
Hope is kindled as your Resurrection shines,
Here in the Eucharist all that is yours becomes mine.
Love is quickened in the depths of my heart,
Looking upon Love, O Jesus, the Love that thou art.

Adventus Medius
MIDDLE COMING

 repare my heart, my mind, my all,
To welcome your Presence and hear your call.

The season of Advent has begun,
Where your Church begs for strength to run.
To run the race marked out for us,
As we reflect upon that first Christmas.
You came in humility, a babe in a manger,
Now we await the glorious Second Coming
   of our Savior.

In between these two advents,
We recognize a middle coming in our midst.
You come to us in every Mass,
As you cleanse us from every trespass.
Guilt removed with mercy invoked,
You prepare your Bride to be equally yoked.
She comes down the aisle dressed in white,
To become one flesh with Jesus,
   her strength and might.

The Eucharistic encounter is the middle coming,
Wherein your Bride is nourished
    and prepared for your returning.
Aflame with love till faith be made sight,
Time collapses as dawn is brought to light.

So hasten beloved children of God
    to the Eucharistic feast,
To prepare for the Second Coming where Christ
    will vanquish the evil beast.
Darkness, sin, and gloom do not get the final say,
For that babe in a manger will come again
    on that Judgment Day.

Stay awake and be watchful
    for we do not know the hour,
Pray without ceasing and ready yourself
    for the final encounter.
Eat his flesh and drink his blood,
And your house won't fall in the coming flood.

Throne and Altar

H ungry for the Bread of Life,
Thirsty for the Blood of Christ.
Panting for his Presence,
Eager for God's Essence.
Stripped of all scrupulosity,
Cleansed from all anxiety.

Heart beats stilled,
Breaths gently blowing,
Eyes fixed on Jesus,
The Beloved One is coming.

Pleasing aromas surround,
The twenty-four elders fall down.
Angels sing his praise,
The dead now living set their gaze.
Saints robed in splendor all around,
The cherubim throne causes joy to abound.
The King is seated above the heavens,
Now this Lamb comes as our leaven.

We glimpse his glory,

Mirror dimly lit,
Radiating light,
Through the Church he carefully knit.

Bride yearning for her Groom,
Groom preparing a precious room.
In that room an altar is built,
The altar takes away her guilt.
On this altar his Body he will give,
Blood poured out, the Bride can now live.
Flesh of my flesh, bone of my bone,
The Bridegroom makes the Bride his own.

Divine romance,
O great mystery,
That we now partake
Of Christ's Divinity!

Gazing Through the Veil

Light licks the air,
As the flame of the candles flicker and flare.
Monstrance erect, golden beams ablaze,
With the fire of Divine Love drawing all to gaze.

Eucharist enclosed by sparkling gems,
Jesus looks at me and I look at him.

Veiled glory in my midst,
Eyes of faith get a glimpse.
Humility himself in lowliness clad,
Requiring humility for all to be glad.

Sweet aromas from incense burning,
Mysterious Presence all-consuming.

Gaze transfixed upon my Lord,
Light from Light, the veil is torn.

Mingling with Divinity

Christ's Body and Blood flowing through my veins,
Life enveloped by the God who reigns.
Christ's Soul and Divinity mingling with me,
This union of love sets me free.
Freed from the shackles of shame and sin,
Righteousness gladdens the souls of just men.

Joy is ringing,
As angel choirs are singing.
Longing to look at this grace bestowed,
The angels rejoice as God's plan unfolds.

Hidden before all ages began,
Divine Wisdom decreed to give himself to man.
Though our folly made us flee in terror,
The love of Christ compels us near.

Here he is for all to see,
The Lowly One as fruit from the Tree.
Tree of Life, O Cross of Christ,
Bearing the fruit of Bread Divine,
And Blood under the guise of wine.

Partaking of this Heavenly Feast,
Divine Life grows as bread from yeast.

Body and Blood for all is offered,
God and man are permanently partnered.
Awe-struck we bow before this Mystery,
The Church now called to Life in Holy Trinity.

Bread of Angels

Bread of angels, glory abounds,
Adoring your majesty within the golden shroud.
Longing to look at the grace we consume,
The angelic hosts with incense perfume.
Seraphim so sweet in your love for him,
Cherubim full of knowledge ever-bright, not dim.
Thrones resound God's divine decrees,
Dominions beckon all to fall on their knees.
Virtues give strength for creatures to obey,
Powers thunder what he will say.
Principalities govern the world for God's glory,
Archangels command those enlisted in the Lord's army.
Angels abound, calling all to bow,
Guardians of the little ones drawing near, even now.
All the heavenly hosts are here,
In this tiny chapel where God's Presence is clear.

Hidden yet Here

Hidden yet visible,
Mystical yet concrete,
Time collapses at this hour,
Past pulled to present,
Present pushed to flower.

Memorial makes real,
The Paschal Sacrifice, once for all,
Future glory, our promised pledge,
Staring now at me to hear his splendid call.

Giving hope of Resurrection,
Giving strength to endure my cross,
Words are not enough,
My whole self I offer you, raw and real,
    under no guise of gloss.

O my Jesus, here in your Presence,
My sinful heart is made pure.

O my Jesus, no sweeter Name,
Savior of all, Healer of the lame.

Hidden yet here,
Mystical yet real,
Heaven and earth collided,
Time in adoration, here I have abided.

Eucharistic glory,
Pouring forth in all humility,
Shine on my frail self,
The wondrous splendor of your Divinity.

God, Who Now Appears

hrough him all things are made,
In him all creation is sustained.
The God who formed the fields,
Made the mountains,
And supplied the seas,
Is the God who now appears to me.

Bread of Life given for all,
Silent Presence among the sounds of nature's call.
Birds chirping,
Roosters are crowing,
Cows are mooing,
And the bees are buzzing.
All life now bows before the source,
Bringing adoration to the Blessed Host.

Peru cries out longing for more,
People with good hearts, come and meet your Lord.
Do not remain in ignorance or sin,
But come forth to the merciful I AM.
He is here in your midst,
Your humble hearts will give you a glimpse.

Love and grace are here to be found,
Creation groans for our praise to resound!

Powerful Fragility

ragile babe entrusted to human hands,
Weakness assumed to save mortal man.

Christmas mystery made manifest in the Blessed Host,
With the Magi and all nations,
We declare Jesus as our only boast.

Simple love,
Powerful fragility,
Christ has come,
In all humility.

Show me the path of condescension,
So that one day I may participate in your Ascension.

Love descending,
Man ascending,
A great exchange,
So pure, so bright,
The Most Holy Eucharist before me,
Faith yearning for sight.

If only I understood a little more,
Who it is that I adore,
Trembling in the Presence of Goodness,
My life would find its fullness.

Light of glory shine on me,
Take me up to Heaven with thee.

Wasting Time

asting time with the Author of time
   is no waste of time at all.
   Busyness and productivity are the modern
buzzwords often confused for virtues.
Productivity rooted in peace is the only form
   of productivity worth producing.

Though the world and my flesh might scream
   that I'm wasting my life
By sitting still at the feet of Jesus in the Eucharist, I know
   deep down a secret, that is no secret at all:
Apart from you, Lord Jesus, I can do nothing.

You ask me to abide,
You ask me to be still,
You call me to simply see,
To simply be.

Here I am Lord,
Your servant is listening.

Bearing fruit, multiplying talents, working hard
   for the kingdom,

These things are only possible through you,
    with you, and in you.
Apart from you I can do nothing.
Apart from you I don't want to do anything.

If all I did my whole day,
If all I did my whole life,
Is exchange glances of love with you
    in prayer and adoration,
Then my "wasted" life would have been no waste at all.
For eternal life, the type of life that keeps going,
    that remains,
Is a life of knowing God and Jesus Christ
    whom he has sent.

Life of love in the Holy Trinity, the divine dance of love,
    the exchange of love into which I am called,
This is life, true life.

So, here I am Lord,
Still and silent in your Presence,
Not doing anything yet doing everything.

Eucharist So Sweet

ucharist so sweet, propels us toward the
Unity which we seek.
Christ is present in his Church,
His promise to be with us renews the face of the earth.
Always he is here,
Relishing when we draw near.
I know no greater mystery than our
Savior's sacrifice on display,
Time collapses when Heaven touches earth this way.

Acrostic poem, spelling "Eucharist"

Tortured Love Divine

 ord Divine,
In monstrance enshrined,
Living flesh of God,
Drawing all who wander abroad.
Gift of self for all to see,
Only faith can get a glimpse of thee.
Awaken my heart, awaken my love,
Enrapture me, God, in the life above.
Strengthen my feeble flesh,
Enlighten my mind entangled and enmeshed.
Renew this temple you have made,
My body is yours, the price you've already paid.
Bought me at a price so great,
No money could reverse my doomed fate.
Your own body you gave for mine,
Bloodied and bruised, tortured Love Divine.
How can I not give you all of me,
When on that cross you set me free?
Nourished now on Paschal Mystery,
You make me share in your Divinity.
What joy, what glee, the gift of thee!
You raise me up and help me bear my own bloody tree.

Open Their Eyes

ystically present before my eyes,

Love made manifest produces deep sighs.

I cannot look at you without being struck with awe,

In this place of silence your love is the law.

O Beloved Jesus in the Blessed Host,

Will you not reveal yourself to those I love most?

The Protestant Revolt tore many away,

But isn't reconciliation possible this day?

I long for all to come back to one fold,

That the world may know you,

   and the Christian witness be bold.

The Jesus they preach, the Jesus they love,

Is the one who is here is this Eucharist from above.

Open their eyes,

Cause them to see,

If only they knew,

You are here with me.

Would they not beg to be welcomed by your Church?

Would they not give up every piece of merch?

Surely these beloved children of yours,

Would gladly give up all worldly lures.

You are here in the stillness,

Fulfilling every promise,
To be our nourishment,
Our life and our sweetness.
Mercy made manifest,
Beckons all to come.
At the Eucharistic Feast,
Visible unity shall be won.

Devil's Bane

evil's bane,
Eucharist consumed.
Lion's mane,
Sacrament infused.
Lamb slain,
Sins washed away.
Heart tamed,
Mercy given today.
Demons flee,
Saints rejoice,
Hell-bound man,
Make your choice.
Receive glory,
Exchange your shame,
Gift of immortality,
Marks you with God's Name.
O wondrous Sacrament,
Mercy made manifest,
O splendid Presence,
Grace that is finest.

With & Without You

The brightness of your light,
Casts out the darkest night.
Conquering hero in meekness shown,
For you the Holy Spirit within me groans.
Still with us since times ancient,
You are so kind, gentle, and patient.
Waiting for all people to repent,
For the salvation of sinners, you were sent.
Same yesterday, today, and forever,
O Jesus, let our friendship grow and not sever.
My life is in your hands,
Your breath follows me across distant lands.
Without you I am dust,
With you, I am just.
Without you there is no life,
With you, there's an end to strife.
Without you my world is confused,
With you, peace is pursued.
O Immanuel still with us under guise of bread,
Making all the difference in the paths we tread.
Transforming grace so gracefully infused,
Sinful humanity no longer accused.

Holiness now possible with your life taking root,
With you in our souls we bear much fruit.
So, let your Presence always remain,
Through you in me, expand your reign.

Joy in God's Marvelous Work

ullness of joy in your Presence,
Your heart laid before me ravishes my own,
Feelings of love fire through my soul,
Deep yearnings for others to partake of your Presence,
Grips me deep within my bones.
O what joy when others come to see
    the truth of the Eucharist,
Your Presence still with us.
Words cannot describe,
This mystery so sublime.
All people long for this encounter,
Though many don't know to look at the Catholic Church,
The Church which you are the Founder.
Witnesses arise,
Let the world see you shine,
With Eucharistic glow,
The world will come to know.
The Catholic Church is God's own Bride,
All will have joy if they lay down their pride.
Flocks of people will come into this Sacred Family,

The Holy Spirit is working to restore Christian unity.

Eyes fixed on Jesus,

Source of all joy,

Locked eyes never waver,

Steadfastness we employ.

A marvelous work is being done,

Let us join God, who is on the run.

He runs to every human heart,

Knocking at the door of every sort.

So, open up,

He comes to sup,

Bread made Body,

Wine made Blood,

Drink, Beloved, from the Sacred Cup.

Be that
Eucharistic Presence

Eucharist consumed,
Causes a sacrificial life to bloom.
God with us in this way,
Compels us to accompany others every day.
Nourished by this Sacrament,
Beckons us to live the way Jesus meant.
Our life lived with and for others,
Is a Eucharistic life no foe can smother.
Love so attractive, Love so Divine,
When we bear the fruit of this Eucharist sublime.
Though others may not know,
Why we carry this Eucharistic glow,
We display for all we meet,
The Image of Christ who longs to wash their feet.
So, come my fellow Catholics,
Transformed by the Blessed Sacrament,
Let us go forth and be,
That Eucharistic Presence for all to see.

I Love You Jesus

I love you Jesus,
With all I have, I love you.
You are my best friend,
My Lord and my God,
My companion on life's journey,
My all and my everything.
Words cannot do justice to my love for you,
Yet this is only a feeble response to your love for me.
I have not been crucified for you,
Tortured for you,
Scorned for you.
But you first loved me,
Crucified for me,
Tortured for me,
Scorned for me.
Rising victorious with forgiveness on your lips,
You raised me to new life in Baptism,
And our friendship commenced.
Yet even before then, you knew me,
In my mother's womb you knit me together,
With the purest of love.
As the years went by and our friendship deepened,

My longing for you was only strengthened.
Alas you did something I did not expect,
You revealed your Church to me,
And by so doing, you opened my eyes to see
Your Incarnational Presence in the Eucharist.
O intimacy so sweet,
O intimacy beyond all telling,
Now at last we are one,
As I partake of your Sacred Body and Blood.
Your life flows in me in whole new ways,
The gift of yourself given to me every single day.
O marvelous mystery,
O sublime Sacrament,
Thank you, Jesus,
I love you Jesus!

Simple Beauty, Sublime Reality

imple beauty,
Sublime reality,
Eucharist Divine,
Your holiness becomes mine.
Transformed by your Body and Blood,
Grace comes in me like a flood.
Sacrifice so sweet,
Heaven and earth meet.
Mangled on the Cross,
Tortured for all of us.
Raised in glory to God's right hand,
Ascension opens our passage to new land.
Prophets foretold, but could not have guessed,
The Lamb slain, purchased our eternal rest.
Now present among us in the Eucharistic Bread,
New Manna from Heaven dispels all dread.
Partaking of God's very life,
Ends all human strife.
United in the one Body of our Lord,

Plowshares of love replace our bloodied sword.

Loving as he loved,

The new commandment given,

Filled with Christ's life,

Our love becomes leaven.

O beauty so simple,

O reality so sublime,

When I partake of Jesus,

All that is his becomes mine.

Our Father in Heaven

Our Father in heaven
  revealed by the Son come down,
  Restoring the holiness of God's Name,
 so his holiness would resound.
The King spread the Kingdom all around,
The Kingdom in the midst of our silent sound.
"Not my will, but yours be done,"
Jesus taught us full surrender,
Commending his spirit to the Father most tender.
Our daily Bread given each day in Mass,
His Body broken and Blood poured out to the last.
As he cried forgiveness for his foes,
So we forgive all people far and close.
The standard of the Cross leads us away from temptation,
We must embrace the pain of Christ with every sensation.
The Devil defeated by the Blood of the Lamb,
Evil is vanquished when we run into him.
The Kingdom, the power, and the glory are yours,
We cry the "Amen" amidst the angel scores.

Still My
Anxious Heart

till my anxious heart, O Lord.
In the stillness of your Eucharistic Presence,
Calm my every nerve,
Fix my thoughts on you,
Let me not be distracted or disturbed.
Forge our friendship in the silence.
Restful abiding is my portion,
Consume my very being,
Let me lean my head on your chest,
Let me glimpse the love in your eyes.
Still my anxious heart,
Replace it with your own.
As I ponder your ways,
And meditate on your Word,
My thoughts are captured by your love.
Help me to receive,
Not to grasp or overthink.
Help me to abide,
Not to carry the weight of the world.

Help me to be still in your stillness,
Silent in your silence,
With you in your Presence.
This is my call,
This is my home,
At rest on your chest,
Near your Eucharistic throne.

Worship What We Consume

ystery sublime,

We worship what we consume,

Christ in us, glory beyond all time.

Worshipping the Eucharist,

Consuming the Eucharist,

Intimacy beyond recall,

Where Christ is all in all.

Leading us to the bosom of the Father,

Through the Holy Spirit,

   we are adopted into this encounter.

O Jesus in the Host,

You are our only boast.

O Jesus on the Altar,

Give us strength not to falter.

O Jesus in the Most Holy Sacrament,

Come in fire upon this mortal tent.

Immanuel then, now, and forever,

We give you glory ever and ever.

Streams of Mercy

treams of mercy pouring,
Heaven's love is roaring.
Generous and kind,
Our good Lord we find.
Eucharist in my sight,
Changing my darkness into light.
Every burden lifted,
Impurities in my heart sifted.
God has washed away my iniquity,
The Sacrament of Penance brings tranquility.
Jesus in the Priest,
Jesus in the Eucharistic Feast.
Immanuel forgives,
My soul now lives.
Thank you, Lord, for your grace,
Grant me perseverance to win this race.
Breathing in your love with every sigh,
I glorify your Name, God Most High.

Irrational Modernity

rrational modernity,
Rationalizing sin,
Darkness grows,
As ink dripping from a pen.
What can help us in this hour?
Who can save us from Satan's shower?
None but you, O Light from Light,
None but you, O Eucharist Delight.
You are Jesus, God and Savior,
You are the Lord, now and forever.
When darkness enshrouds,
Your light penetrates the clouds.
When all seems lost,
You give yourself without cost.
You, O Jesus, secure our stability,
Only in you, we find our identity.
So, to you we look,
To you we cry,
Confident of one thing,
Your Second Coming draws nigh.

Glimpses of Him

oice of God beckons,

Speaking words of wisdom,

"Draw near to this fount of immortality,"

"Come without cost, come with nothing."

Here I am Lord, at your Altar,

Immerse me with the light of your face,

Immerse me in your Presence.

Shades of grey give way to the day,

Night is gone, sin destroyed,

When we come to you,

Physician of Life.

Mirror so dim,

Glimpses of him.

In the poor,

In the sick,

In the weary worker,

In the busy mother,

In the Eucharist.

These glimpses and hints,

Foretastes of future romance.

I come, I bow,

Give sight to my faith,

Catch me up in glory now.

All angels and saints in joyful silence in this place,

Heaven mingled with earth,

Mortality gives way to the true Life.

Joy and happiness within,

Erupts at every glimpse of him.

Resurrection joy is mine,

When the cross I carry becomes refined.

Refined in the fires of Divine Love,

With Christ, in Christ,

My below is swept up above.

Thank you, Jesus, with me you remain,

Abiding in you is the only way to be sane.

I love you beyond words can tell,

You love me and freed me from my shell.

In you I find myself,

The self that must be emptied,

To find true meaning.

You are my purpose, my hope, my all,

Before you, with angels, I fall.

Grasping for air at the sight of your gaze,

My blindness is lifted out of the haze.

True knowledge, wisdom, and treasures beyond compare,

When I sit in your Presence without a single care.

You are my goal, my life, my all,
Before you, with saints, I fall.
I am yours without reserve,
From temptation and evil please preserve.
If I take my eyes off you,
I'm lost, confused, and chaotic,
With you, I'm found, clear, and at peace,
Not afraid of the demonic.
Crushed them you have,
Crush them you will,
Through Mary's feet and mine,
Satan will be shown without a spine.
O Eucharist, my glory,
O Jesus, my love,
Hell trembles in fear,
Heaven trembles for joy,
I tremble in your goodness,
Knowing you are here.

Confidence Unshakeable

Clarity and confidence,
Oft shaken in a world of uncertainty,
Shines all the clearer when your Eucharistic smile,
Smiles down on me.
I am your servant and slave,
In this posture I am bold and brave.
Clouds of confusion disappear,
When I see you so so near.
Joy uncontainable,
My soul breaks forth in song,
Yet intermingled with sorrow,
As the world's night grows long.
Foes from every side press in,
Yet at peace I remain undimmed.
In you, my Jesus, my Rock,
I stand unshaken,
Confident and clear,
At every hour of earth's clock.

Mary's Tender Gaze

ary praying beside me, looking upon her Son,
Her tender gaze of love helps me
glimpse the Majestic One.
His imminence so profound,
My knees fall to the ground.
Jesus smiles at me,
In the light of faith, I see.
All worries and all cares are gone,
As I look upon the Father's Son.
The Son only does what the Father does,
The Father is here and so is the Son.
Holy Trinity within,
Holy Trinity around,
Enraptured in this love profound.
My heart is flooded with mercy and love,
When I contemplate God with my Mother above.

Sacrifice So Sweet

acrifice so sweet,
Perpetual offering so pleasing,
What prophets proclaimed in shadows,
Full picture now complete.

Holy Sacrifice of the Mass,
Making present Christ's Calvary,
Two thousand years later,
The Church still nourished by the Supper Last.

One sacrifice, all are drawn,
Cross and Eucharist,
Where our Lord gives himself completely,
For the Father and for his Bride to be made one.

O Sacrificial Victim, Priest and Lamb,
Slaughtered in plain sight,
God's Son bearing our iniquity,
Overcoming darkness with his light.

Death passes over,
Life unleashed for all,

Grave is conquered,
An incense of prayer now arises,
So pleasing to the Father.

Sacrifice so sweet,
Manifested at every Mass,
The Bride now nourished,
In this Eucharistic Feast.

Love That Suffers

I n a love that suffers,
    Suffering is conquered.
    In the Christ who was crucified,
Crucifixion leads to life.

O Triumph of the Cross,
Salvation is won,
For in our suffering,
We suffer with the Resurrected One.

On display for all to see,
This Eucharistic sacrifice ever-present with me.

All fears dispelled as death was trampled,
What ought cause us dread,
Only garners us more intimacy with God,
He's redeemed it all because he rose from the dead.

Everything in life now bursts forth with meaning,
And in each moment, on my Beloved, I am leaning.

Rejoice in trial, affliction, and suffering,
All of this can now be united,
To Christ's pure offering.

Darkness of Doubt

When the darkness of doubt creeps in,
The light of faith begins to dim.
The sickness must be cured,
Or to hell, I will be lured.

O Medicine Divine,
Sweet Eucharist sublime,
Come to my aid,
Make all my doubts fade.

Strengthen, O Jesus, my child-like trust,
That I may rest and not let faith rust.

How can I evade these doubts?
Lowliness and humility will give me clout.
For you give grace to the humble,
But make the proud foolishly bumble.

So, here I am assured of your Presence,
You spoke, I believed, this is faith's essence.

Abide in Christ

bide in Christ,
Remain in him,
Fruitfulness will flow,
Your light won't dim.

How to do this?
What does he say?
"Eat my Flesh and drink my Blood,"
His life in you will stay.

God is love,
So, we must love.
When we love, we abide,
And our spirits soar like eagles above.

We love because he loved first.

Receive his total gift of self,
In this Eucharist Feast,
His grace will strengthen you,
And love will rise like yeast.

Monstrance Throne

earlessness is mine,
When I gaze on Jesus in the Eucharist Divine.

Suffering now riddled with meaning,
Death now a gateway to glory exceeding.

When all seems lost,
Christ's strength takes hold.
When darkness surrounds,
The Light shines bold.

O sweet medicine of immortality,
Consume me in my totality.
Penetrate my being with your love,
And rest your Spirit on me like a dove.

Fire of charity, coursing through my veins,
I can't help but love, when Jesus clearly reigns.
Veiled in humble form,
The King is reigning from his monstrance throne.

I see Jesus and Jesus sees me,
All is calm before the throne of him who sets me free.

Mirror Dimly Grows Dimmer

When the mirror dimly lit grows dimmer still,
When chaos surrounds and diseases kill,
We, your People, called by your Name,
Will praise you amidst this purgative flame.

When the world is overrun by fear,
And your Presence seems to disappear,
We remember your covenant so full of love,
And we cling closely to the Christ from above.

Silent prayers shouting towards heaven,
Your Presence still abounds as the new leaven.
Screams of terror fall to a whisper,
As your peaceful Presence consumes our interior.

O Lord, give us strength to persevere,
The oil we've stored up makes us draw near.
Without you all hope is lost,
And all spring warmth turns back to winter frost.

*Written on March 16th, 2020, in the Presence of Jesus Christ in the Eucharist during Adoration in the midst of the coronavirus pandemic when public Mass was not offered.

No Eucharist, No Life

I miss you, my Jesus,

Though I see you now in the monstrance,

I am deprived of partaking of your Presence at Mass.

Mass is cancelled to the public,

Viral disease and viral fear,

Grip the globe in pandemic.

Where can I go?

What can I do?

No Eucharist, no Life.

I am dying,

I am starving,

I am dwindling into nothing.

Yet you have not left,

You do not abandon your chosen ones.

Spiritually, you draw near,

Your covenant of love is strengthened through prayer.

The oil of prayer shall burn all the brighter,

As my hunger for your Presence turns into fire.

This Lenten desert will end,

And this trial shall cease,

Sorrow will give way to joy,

Even if it is piece by piece.

Fire-tried Faith

ire-tried faith,
Purified by flame.
Purgation has begun,
For those called by your Name.

We suffer, but not alone,
With the Lamb slain,
We are pierced, and yet enthroned.

Imagining you with me is no illusion,
For your Word provides encounters with the Living God,
And is certain.

Gripped by grace,
Less tangible it seems,
Yet our distance in the visible,
Can be strengthened by practices spiritual.

So, praying to the Father, as I see Jesus in the Host,
My cries will reach the ears of him who loves us most.

Come, Holy Spirit,

With the fire of your love.
Consume this Temple,
With your Presence from above.

You, great Paraclete,
Wash me, head to feet.
Let me hear your voice,
In this wilderness where I have no choice.

Tangibly Reunited

O my Jesus, how I've missed you.
At last, we are tangibly reunited
   in Eucharistic Adoration.
Long days and nights in quarantine
   left me hungering for your Presence.
Yet, your grace sustained me through it all
   and I am filled with elation.

Now at last, things are not yet normal,

Yet, more grace is given as perseverance is required.

Thank you for this precious trial,

Where endurance turns into character and character into
   hope, hope that can be admired.

Each day in prayer,

Steers our hearts away from fear.

Each day of yearning,

Consumes our hearts with charity burning.

Apart from you I can do nothing.

Whatever trials lay ahead, I know your love surrounds.

Whatever comes my way, I will preach the Gospel
   with joyful sounds.

Source of All Goodness

Source of all goodness,
O Eucharist Most Holy.
Stream of endless gladness,
O Sacrament Divine.
Immortal life so near,
O Emmanuel forever.

Spirit and Fire
Piercing My Soul

oy exploding, in monstrance contained,
Humility enduring, with us you've remained.
Smile of God, glancing through glass,
I delight in your forgiveness of every trespass.

Spirit and fire piercing my soul,
Intimacy divine has become my only goal.

Sheer grace and goodness staring me down,
Wisdom of God declaring in every town.
Will people listen to the Bread of Life?
Will people be united and end their strife?

All evil will pass, and darkness will turn,
Goodness will conquer, and the light will burn.

Your Eucharistic People will carry your Presence,
In word and deed, we draw all to your Essence.
Fragrance of Christ, so sweet to the saints,
Fragrance of Christ, leading us down the narrow way.
Burn within our hearts, Charity Divine,
Sustain us with your Eucharist, intimacy sublime.

O Sacred Heart of Jesus

Sacred Heart of Jesus, pierced with a lance,
O Sacred Heart of Jesus, from which blood
and water flowed,
O Sacred Heart of Jesus, burning with love
from your monstrance throne.

Pierced by my sin,
Returning mercy instead of vengeance,
Your Sacred Heart, O Lord, is the cleansing balm for all
my wretchedness.

Inflamed with Love,
Your Heart consumes me,
In the Most Holy Eucharist,
Your love courses through me.

Alive forever, your Heart is victorious,
Satan's cold breath of death lies dead in the tomb,
Now all the saints rejoice as your life has resumed.

O Sacred Heart of Jesus,
Love so tender and true.
We adore you with our hearts,
Full of love and zeal for you.

Warrior's Strength

Weapons of light,
Given to fight.
Eucharistic prayer,
Drives away all fear.

Angelic hosts adore,
Saints in Heaven bow before.
The Lamb who was slain,
Has become Satan's bane.

Demons tremble in terror,
When the Holy Ones pray without fear.
Perfect love drives darkness away,
Perfect light is here to stay.

O sweet Eucharist, warrior's strength,
Food for soldiers who battle at length.
Humility is infused,
The Enemy is confused.
Mary's soldiers unite,
Bearing Christ, the source of light.

Sacred Silence

 sacred silence,
Where God is found.
O Sacred Host,
Where love abounds.

Quiet stillness,
God's Mystery in fullness.
Presence among us,
Faith perceives thus.

Gentle whispers from above,
Calms every confusion and becomes our salve.
Sweet serenity all-embracing,
Peace is given as we keep on gazing.

O sacred silence,
Where God is found.
Too often neglected,
By the world around.

Jesus, to our senses concealed,
Jesus, in faith revealed.
Here you are, Immanuel forever,
Your promise stands firm, you forsake us never.

Humility Incarnate

H umility incarnate,
Self-emptying love made present.
Christ the King born in feeding trough,
Bread of Life descending in circumstances rough.

Body given,
Blood poured out.
Lamb of God risen,
Paschal sacraments end our drought.

Humility of God astounds,
Awe fills the meek,
The proud, he confounds.

All are welcomed to the marriage feast,
Humble eyes of faith, the only way to see.

Reflect on God's humility,
And reverence will consume you.
Partake of Christ the Eucharist,
And humility will fill you.

Peace So Perfect

eace so perfect,
Mercy so deep,
When I stare at your face,
My heart begins to leap.

O great mystery, if only I understood,
The miracle of miracles,
God's life given as food.

How can it be that my senses don't perceive?
Yet faith in me is confident, that it is Jesus I see.

Peaceful Presence, the leaven of life,
Beyond appearances, your truth pierces like a knife.

I know you are here,
No doubt in my mind.
Your word is sure,
My faith is not blind.

Gift of faith, most treasured gift,
Nourished by Scriptures and saints,

My heart begins to lift.

I'm lifted to heights of contemplation,
Hitherto unimagined.
The gift of yourself really available,
None can fathom.

Transfigured

ransfigured humanity veiled as bread,
Future glory foretasted,
In Communion we are fed.

Unseen glory surrounds this place,
The humility of God,
Unleashes grace.

Angels sing and saints rejoice,
The small still whisper of Love,
Echoing as God's voice.

Past, present, and future, transfixed on the Lamb,
Total self-offering of Jesus,
Brings God to man.

O Bread of Life, transforming all,
Sons and daughters,
Race toward the Father's call.

Fragile humanity caught up in infinity,
Partakers of Divine Nature,
God's People transfigure.

Gift of the Son

No greater gift can be given than
the Father's gift of his only Son.
A father's love for his son surpasses all imagination,
And the Father sent his Son for sinners and their salvation.
The gift that was given many years ago,
Is now given anew at every Mass in the Holy Eucharist.
You give your Son as food for your People,
Nourished on his Body, Blood, Soul, and Divinity,
We come to share in the love of the Most Holy Trinity.
Sons in the Son we become,
And you transform us to be a gift in the Son.
As you sent Jesus,
So you send us,
To the Cross we freely go,
That your abundant love, all may know.

Gaze of Love

aze of love piercing my soul,
Your delight in me, God, is beyond all I know.
As I look into your face in the golden monstrance,
The radiance of your humility sends me into a trance.
O ecstasy untold,
Your Presence here.
The King of Glory,
Draws ever near.
Not worthy to be in this place,
Not worthy to see your face,
Yet, with your life infused,
I kneel transfigured into the likeness of you.
Sublime grace and unconditioned love,
The Bridegroom united with his Beloved.
Thank you, Jesus, for remaining with us,
Your People praise you for your gift so marvelous.

Transform My Clay

neeling before your monstrance throne,
Your goodness invades my every bone.
I tremble with joy in your Presence,
As I contemplate your Eucharistic Essence.

God with us, to the end of the age,
The Breaking of Bread makes the Devil rage.
O Sweetness of Saints,
O Divine Simplicity,
O Eucharistic Lord,
Never leaving, never forsaking, source of my felicity.

Your Church radiates life within,
The hearts of the faithful, treasure the hidden.

Falling on my face, I adore,
Your blessing and grace, I do implore,
Your Presence gives me strength each day,
O Eucharist Most Holy, transform my clay.

Earth Quaking

arth quaking,
Trees trembling,
Seas roaring,
Mountains collapsing,
Creation groans for transfiguration,
Your Presence in the Eucharist is our hope,
For complete transformation.
In the stillness you speak,
From the lowest low to the tallest peak.
Your mercy and goodness flood the world,
You yourself are the great prized pearl.
With all of creation,
Angels and saints,
We bow before you, the One Artist,
Our stories, you paint.

Love, Life, and Light

ove, life, and light, floods my soul,

Waves of glory drip from Jesus's stole.

Great High Priest and Victim so sweet,

Our Lord Jesus Christ gives himself as food to eat.

Living Flesh of Love,

Divinizes all who come.

At the Altar of the Church,

We experience our rebirth.

Heaven's light illumines our way,

As we kneel before the Lamb who was slain.

Golden monstrance bears the sign,

That God is with us to the end of time.

O mysterious Presence of Christ,

You still every storm and all strife.

All burdens you take as your own,

As we bow before your monstrance throne.

Light of the world this day draws near,

Our daily Bread given under the earthly mirror.

Face-to-face right now by fides,

One day we will see clearly, and to that end, you lead us.

Eyes of Humility See

yes of humility see,
The proud remain in misery.
Eucharistic God in so vulnerable a state,
Jesus, the baby, remains here, early and late.

O humble God, what joy you bring,
Dashing pride, the angels sing.
Feeding us with your very self,
Books could not contain this glory on largest shelf.

Humility divine, sweet melody of love,
Flowing to earth from Heaven above.
Glimpses of glory radiate through gold,
Your humble monstrance throne makes us bold.

Lowly Lord entrusted to us,
Lowly people, adore him you must.
Perseverance is needed in these dark times,
Only Eucharistic Light permeates and shines.

Eucharist Here

Eucharist,
So sweet,
Intimacy so sublime,
Sitting near your feet,
You say you are mine.

Fathomless love penetrating my heart,
Stillness makes me hear,
Lord of all,
Always near,
Here.

Priceless Pearl

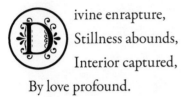ivine enrapture,
Stillness abounds,
Interior captured,
By love profound.

Pouring forth your Blood,
Redemption is mine,
Cleansing sinful mind,
Now I am thine.

For all the world,
Body given,
Your chosen ones reverence,
This priceless pearl.

Sacred Host, My Only Boast

Sacred Host,
You are my boast.
Presence of God everywhere,
Manifested Presence specifically here.
Divine infusion,
Set enemies in confusion.
The saint's refrain,
And Satan's bane.
O Eucharist Most Holy,
I live for you solely.

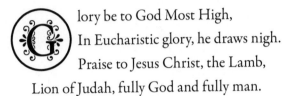

Glory Be to God Most High

Glory be to God Most High,
In Eucharistic glory, he draws nigh.
Praise to Jesus Christ, the Lamb,
Lion of Judah, fully God and fully man.

Infinite Majesty on Heaven's throne,
The Breaking of the Bread makes him known.

God of glory through whom all things were made,
Here with us in the monstrance you have laid.
O Mystery of Mysteries,
Never-ending source of grace,
When God became man,
Man could behold your face.
Face so hidden, yet so present,
Now under guise of bread,
All things bitter become pleasant.

Pledge of future glory, this Holy Communion,
Souls mingled with God, in complete and indissoluble union.

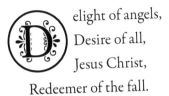

Delight of Angels

Delight of angels,
Desire of all,
Jesus Christ,
Redeemer of the fall.

Choirs of Heaven,
Surrounding the monstrance,
Joy is exploding,
Sinners gain entrance.

O joy of Heaven,
On earth we adore,
Appearance like bread,
But it is God we implore.

Winged spirits united,
In celestial praise,
Man kneels before the Eucharist,
And our hearts are set ablaze.

Like Children We Come

ike children we come,
Believing your simple word,
"This is my Body."
Not "like" your Body,
Not a "symbol" of your Body,
But, yes, your very Body.

O Body of Christ!
Encapsulating the fullness of Divinity,
Indeed, in the Host we experience all,
Body, Blood, Soul, and Divinity.

Fountain of life,
Source of love,
Grace unquenchable,
Joy unspeakable,
Humility most manifest,
This day your children,
Call you blessed.

Our Father

Our Lord Jesus Christ, present in our midst,
Father of all, sent his Son
            to rescue man from the abyss.
Who are we that God would love us?
Art mere mortals worthy of this glory?
In the depths of our hearts the Holy Trinity resides,
Heaven awakens and beckons our dead selves to rise.
Hallowed among the nations, God's Name proclaimed,
Be glory, splendor, and honor, God's Name is famed.
Thy Word goes forth like wildfire,
Name above all names, Jesus our one desire.

Thy scepter is a scepter of righteousness,
Kingdom of Heaven undoing all injustice.
Come, O King, and rule in our hearts,

Thy majesty consumes every thought of ours.
Will you withhold your Presence today?
Be it not so, or else we will turn back into clay.
Done is the past gone before,
On this day we rejoice in your Presence forevermore.
Earth is shaken with Heaven's dew,

As we behold the Eucharist, we behold you.
It is a never-ending mystery, a continual contemplation.
Is God manifested through transubstantiation?
In the Sacred Host, we see God, our only boast,
Heaven is here because God has drawn near.

Give this Eucharistic medicine,
Us sinners you give,
This divine gift.
Day begets day, and now we live.
Our Lord is Light,
Daily we receive,
Bread from Heaven, glory in us conceived.

And for all of this we still stumble and fall,
Forgive us everything we have done wrong.
Us sinners come back to you,
Our transgressions fall, and for you we long.
Trespasses forgiven,
As we confess your Name,
We partake of your Presence,
Forgive the times we've shown you disdain.
Those who wait for the Lord shall be saved.
Who dares to refuse you honor?

Trespass of trespasses, the pride of man,
Against this pride you give yourself as Bread.
Us partakers of your Presence,
   redeemed by your Blood that was shed.

And let us go rejoicing to your throne,
Lead us to your restful home.
Us sinners are saved,
Not by our own,
Into your Presence we come,
Temptation disappears as we know we are not alone.

But seeing the battle that lies ahead,
Deliver us Lord from the serpent's bed.
Us delighters of God,
From us drive that ancient foe,
Evil is conquered, as the Eucharist is sown.

Amen, Amen, let it be done unto us
   according to your word.

Each starting word is a word of the "Our Father" prayer. New stanza occurs for each of the seven petitions of the "Our Father" prayer.

Basking in Beatitude

asking in beatitude,
O happiness sublime,
Every glance from Jesus,
Enkindles love refined.

Spirit and fire in this subtle form,
Eucharistic glory perfects every norm.

Grace begets grace,
As I stare at the Host,
My body trembles,
As I'm filled with the Holy Ghost.

Golden gleam, from you all holiness streams,
Monstrance throne, penetrates my bones.

Truth in person,
Exchange of love made possible,
When the priest consecrates the bread,
The Word made flesh now visible.

Consumed by your gift,

The very gift of yourself,
All people from every nation,
In loving adoration have knelt.

Name above all names,
Most Holy Name of Jesus,
Savior of mankind,
In the Eucharist you have freed us.

Eucharist

ucharist Most Holy,

Union with God achieved.

Christ among his People,

Heart of love perceived.

Awe begets awe,

Reverence is due to your Name.

Isolation is demolished,

Sins are shed,

True Presence of Christ accomplished.

*Acrostic poem, spelling "Eucharist"

Dewdrops of Grace

 ewdrops of grace falling upon bread,
Words of the priest transubstantiate,
Now with Christ's Body we are fed.

Calvary made present,
Sacrifice renewed.
Resurrection glory,
Makes all things new.

Super-essential Bread,
On this our lives depend,
Apart from Christ we can do nothing,
With him, everything.

O Mystery Divine,
Sweet Sacrament sublime,
Transfigure us this day,
Divinize this clay.

Christin Me

hrist in me,
Christ before me,
Christ all around me.

Through him,
With him,
In him.

All creation held together,
All creation groaning together,
Renewed creation foreshadowed in Eucharistic glory,
Any storm can now be weathered.

Presence of God everywhere,
Manifested in monstrance here.
Drawing near I let go of fear,
Merciful grace wipes away every tear.

Death and destruction give way to grace,
Life and light conquers all,
I kneel amazed, on you I gaze.

Christ in me, the hope of glory,
Worshipping you, whom I have just consumed,
Love and holiness begin to bloom.

Seed of the Kingdom now implanted within,
Signs and wonders burst forth,
The fruit of knowing him.

Christ my glory, Christ my strength,
With you in me, I will persevere,
Whatever life's length.

Even Now

Even now, you have given me yourself.
Even now, your gaze is fixed on me.
I tremble with joy in your Presence.
I shake with love in my innermost being.

Amidst the darkness covering the earth, you bring light.
Amidst the sorrow and decay, you bring gladness and life.
O Sacred and Eucharistic Heart of Jesus
   be with us to the end.
O Sacred and Eucharistic Heart of Jesus
   I love you as a friend.

Pangs of Hunger

Pangs of hunger for your Presence,
My whole being longs for your Essence.
Infused in my body,
Your Eucharistic glory.
Quenching all thirst,
My hunger is stilled,
Contemplating your Presence,
All sin is killed.

Holiness radiates,
From the monstrance you've embraced.
Your little home within the Church,
Gives hope to all for Resurrection birth.

Exposed on the Altar,
Laid bare before men,
Your sacrifice renewed,
Love conquers all sin.

You are life,
You are joy,
You end all strife,
You employ all hope, all goodness, all beauty.

O Father, make your face shine on us,
Through this Eucharistic Heart of Jesus.

Peace in Your Presence

eace in your Presence,
All chaos is stilled.
Peace in your Presence,
All emptiness is filled.

At the beginning of creation,
    you brought light to the dark,
Now in redemption,
    you bring light through Peter's barque.

O peaceful Presence,
Eucharist Divine,
Fill my Body,
With intimacy sublime.

Flowering love blossoms in my soul,
As I contemplate your face,
In this monstrance bowl.

Rivers of peace flow from your pierced side,
O wonderful sacraments,
Encounters with God I find.

Peace in your Presence,
Unending peace.
Peace in your Presence,
Love unleashed.

Resting Amidst Chaos

Resting amidst chaos,
Jesus lay in the boat.
Resting amidst chaos,
Jesus lays in the monstrance cloak.

Disciples fearful, forget their faith,
The God who created all,
Is always with them,
And can still any storm, and any wave.

O forgetful sheep, be not afraid,
The Lord of all is walking on the waves.

Let me rest with you Jesus,
In the depths of the boat,
Let me rest with you Jesus,
When darkness seems to gloat.

Triumphal rest shows forth our trust,
In the Father's love, rest we must.

Filled with God

otal self,
Given today.
Blood of God,
Pumping through my veins.

Inebriated by love,
Intoxicated with peace,
Eucharistic glory,
Makes all striving cease.

Filled with God,
All things are possible.
Divinity shared,
Makes me walk through crucibles.

Gift of Jesus, given today.
How can we not trust every word he will say?
If God has not spared his one and only Son,
Will he withhold anything from his little ones?

Stamp of Love,
Seal of Goodness,
Bread of Life,
Makes us know God's nearness.

Mercy Made Manifest

espite our sinfulness,
God is still with us.
Mercy made manifest,
By your Presence in the Eucharist.

You have not abandoned us,
Though we do not deserve you.
The godless world so blind,
Seems to have rejected the good and true.

Though we are faithless,
You remain faithful.
To the end of the age,
You are with us, and your children are thankful.

Mercy made manifest,
In every Catholic Church.
Wherein your Eucharist is given,
And humanity has rebirth.

Now it is time for your Church to shine,
To remain in you with our hearts refined.

To give you the glory that is due,
Hallow your Name in us, with saints in every pew.

All glory to the God above,
His mercy transforms our lowly love.
All glory to the God of all mercy,
Our sinfulness is drowned in his merciful sea.

Living Flesh of Love

Presence permeating every part of me,
My blinded eyes now clearly see.
Though veiled under the appearance of bread,
The Living Flesh of Love is here, he is no longer dead.

Eyes of love, piercing my soul,
Gaze of beauty, I feel your pull.
Jesus Christ, living and true,
Death is conquered for me and you.

O Living Flesh of Love,
The one who descended from above.
Now at the right hand of Majesty,
Transcending Presence of Christ for all to taste and see.

Eucharist Most Holy

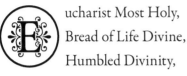ucharist Most Holy,
Bread of Life Divine,
Humbled Divinity,
Presence of God sublime.

Body and Blood of Christ,
Living Flesh of Love,
True Manna from Heaven,
Sustenance from above.

Way-farers Bread,
Life to the dead,
Incarnate reality,
Infused Divinity.

Satan's bane,
The torture of demons,
Lion's mane,
The soldier's summons.

Warrior Pilgrim's strength,
Might of God consumed,

O Eucharist Most Holy,
Making saints to bloom.

Heaven's glory,
Gift to earth,
O Eucharist Most Holy,
Renewal of rebirth.

Thanksgiving sacrifice,
Fragrant offering to the Father,
O Eucharist Most Holy,
Uniter of sister and brother.

Cause of joy,
Source of all hope,
Resurrection glory,
Handed down through every Pope.

Sacrament of Sacraments,
Jesus Christ himself,
O Resurrected Flesh of God,
Fountain of Love, the total gift of self.

Grace Now Pours

Worshipping that which was consumed,
Fragile humanity, now Heaven assumes.
Glory of God radiating through my body,
Beholding the source of all that is holy.

Creation bows,
Angels rejoice,
Him who was slain,
Now risen to reign.

King of all goodness,
Your Presence among us,
Humility has triumphed,
Lowly ones victorious.

Empowered by grace,
Always seeking your face,
Children of God,
Live to give you laud.

All glory, honor, and power are yours,
Through this Holy Eucharist all grace now pours.

Fear Flees, Your Presence I Breathe

ear flees,
Your Presence, I breathe.
Death destroyed,
Grace deployed.

Suffering swept away,
As the Cross gives way,
To Resurrection reality,
On that Sacred Sunday.

Redemption wrought,
My sinful soul now bought.
Precious Blood given,
Your life in me livin'.

With this Sacred Feast,
The saints conquer the Beast.
Word of their story,
Blood of the Lamb,

Offering their lives,
Accuser now banned.

Fear flees,
Your Presence, I breathe.
No longer a slave,
Because Jesus conquered the grave.

Love Leaps

Love leaps in my heart,
Your many blessings abound,
Flowing from the Most Holy Sacrament,
Love pours forth profound.

Glimpsing grace when I see your face,
Veiled, yet present,
Faith makes your Presence apparent.

Raging waves of the world fall silent,
As the silent calm of your stillness permeates the air.
Lifting all my burdens,
You become my only care.

O Jesus, meek and humble,
Still with us to the end,
Your sacrifice on the Cross,
Still bearing fruit on every Altar.
As we participate in this sacrifice,
Our love for you does not falter.

O sweet Jesus, enrapture me once more,
Never let me forget your saving Presence,
Saving me from myself, by giving me life in the veil torn.

The More
I'm with You

Lord,
The more I'm with you,
The more I want to be with you.
My feelings are nothing compared with your own.
When you ascended to God's right hand, you didn't just
disappear to your throne.
You gave us your Spirit and remained with us yourself.
Through the Sacrament of the Altar, we experience your
gift of self.
Yes, Jesus, you are still with us,
Present in the Eucharist,
Present in the poor,
Present in the faithful,
Present in every heart that opens the door.
You did not leave us, but remained with us.
You like us. You actually like us.
Your Ascension simply makes your Incarnation extend,
To the very end.
Head and Body now one, Bride and Bridegroom united.
One flesh union,

In every Holy Communion,

Strengthens the marriage bond, indissolubly ignited.

Thank you, Lord, for the Supper of the Lamb,

Foretasted now in the Eucharist,

Generously given through your Apostles' hands.

O Sacrament Most Holy,

O Sacrament Divine,

Grant me intimacy with you,

Intimacy sublime.

Gift of Life

 ift of Life,
 Ending all strife.
 Source of peace,
Captives released.

Blood and water flowing,
Resurrection Life outpouring.
Old self now crucified,
New life is vivified.

Eucharist so sweet,
Quickening my feet,
To spread the Good News,
And fill the empty pews.

Jesus is here,
Let enemies beware,
The humble King is alive,
Fear and death have died.

Tried and true, your Presence remains,
Urging us forward, to the end of days.
Now we see, and grasp in part,
One day face-to-face, new glory will start.

Sustenance So Sweet

orking all things for our good,
You have become our daily food.
Sustenance so sweet,
Every morning you are eager to meet.

Why so eager?
Why so excited?
Why so faithful?
Why so enlivened?

Source of goodness,
In you is our happiness.
Faithful to the end,
You call us your friend.

O friendship of Jesus, nothing compares,
I'm friends with God, his Divinity he shares.
Partaking Christ's Presence,
I'm flooded with his Essence.
Intimately united,
My love for him ignited.

All-consuming fire flowing in my veins,
Like the burning bush of old, I still remain.
Consumed yet here,
His Presence so near.

I stand in awe of the King of Kings,
My soul enraptured with love now sings and sings.

Gift of Glory

ift of Glory,
The most glorious of gifts.
Christ's own Presence,
Given in our midst.

We do not deserve anything,
Yet you come to us despite everything.

Gift of Love,
Sacrifice so sweet,
Help us to imitate this love,
In all that we do with our hands and feet.

We come to your grace-filled throne,
Begging you to invade our bones.

Gift of Hope,
Resurrected Body of Christ,
Foretaste of our future,
If we persevere through the miseries of life.

Glory given,

Love now leavened,

Hope enkindled,

Christ in us now mingled.

Lowly yet Reigning

ixing our eyes on your tender gaze,
Your love pierces through our sinful haze.

The muck and mire of worldly gloom,
Slips right off as we contemplate you.

Chains are broken,
Refreshment now given.
The Presence of Christ among us,
Transforms our lowliness,
And grants us holiness.

Lowly yet reigning,
Here yet transcending.
Catch us up in your humility,
And we shall reign with you in life,
And in eternity.

Cocooning

ocooning in the adoration chapel,
Caterpillars turn into butterflies,
Lowly lives reach new heights.
The ugliness of our past,
Is transfigured at last.
Ascending the mountain of God,
Catches us up in his divine love.
Infused with grace,
We see his face.
Becoming what we behold,
Divinization makes us bold.
Remaining creatures, yet consumed by our Lord,
The burning bush of old, is what we have become.
Enflamed with love,
Remolded in Christ,
Creation has been longing for this moment,
When God's sons and daughters embrace the Atonement,
And sacrifice themselves with our Eucharistic Lord.
Becoming transfigured,
Being transformed,
Saints are coming,
Let the world beware.

In silence and in prayer,
From the Eucharistic chapel,
Holiness is unleashed,
Saints are released.

Immanuel

mmanuel,
God with us,
Never forsakes us,
Remains with us.

Here in this place,
Immanuel stays,
Nourishing his Church,
Granting all rebirth.

Still with us,
And to the end,
Our Incarnational God,
Remains forever our friend.

Serene Silence

erene silence shrouds this Sacrament,
Heaven's thunder fills the air,
Cherubim and seraphim sing his praises,
Jesus Christ our Savior draws near.

Sacred silence surrounds this Sacrament,
Heaven's roar now heard in my heart,
Mary and Joseph and all the saints,
Cast crowns of gold toward the Holy One set apart.

Joy Overflows

oy overflows,
Love erupts,
Hope is kindled,
Peace fills my cup.

Goodness, mercy, and grace abound,
When, in your Presence, I know that I'm found.

Kindness quickens in my heart of hearts,
Your gentle gaze causes sin to depart.

O how I love you Jesus,
Your Eucharistic Presence is my joy,
My joy overflows.

Journey of Intimacy

mbarking upon this journey of intimacy,
I am struck by your love that only faith can see.
What looks like bread is actually Jesus,
You give me yourself Lord and hold nothing back.
Each day in Mass, the total gift of yourself is mine,
In all the tabernacles of the world you abide.
Your enduring Presence,
Your constant Presence,
Your immediate and manifest Presence,
Gives me a glimpse of your profound love for your People.
What can we say?
What can we do?
The only proper response is to worship and honor you.

Arms Wide Open

rms wide open to embrace your prodigal children,
The strong squeeze of your hug brings peace to
those who are burdened.

You love us and never stop,
You embrace us and never let go.
Embracing you back,
Arms wide open to receive,
This is your call,
To whom your love is perceived.

I don't want to let you go,
Though sometimes I stray,
The narrow path of love,
Is the only path, the only way.

Cross made present in your Eucharistic Feast,
Strengthens me to embrace you
in the suffering you went through,
All the way to Calvary.

To be glorified with you,
We must suffer with you,
Only the Eucharist can make this burden a gentle yoke,
A certain path for us weakened folk.

Bloodstained Wood

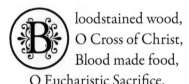loodstained wood,
O Cross of Christ,
Blood made food,
O Eucharistic Sacrifice.

Body and Blood given for me,
Soul and Divinity of Jesus,
Makes me one with the Holy Trinity.

Body, Blood, Soul, and Divinity,
Right before my very eyes.
Source of my faith,
Summit of my life,
Your Eucharistic Presence,
Brings me new life.

Sacrifice so sweet, O sweet Eucharist,
Gift of self,
Gift of love,
Laying down my life,
Willing our good.
Faith sees,
Hope restored,
Love remains,
Abiding forever, Our Savior and Lord.

Leaning into Your Chest

eaning into your chest,
I find my rest.

Peace prevails,
Pervading my person,
Your Presence pervades,
The gift of your Person.

Father sending the Son,
Son made present through the Spirit.
Man's participation in this,
Is his source and summit.

Divinization occurs,
As the Eucharist is consumed.
Even looking at the Host,
Transfiguration comes through the Holy Ghost.

Changed forever into the likeness of Christ,
Partaking this Divine sustenance gives us Divine traits,
And has the power to make us,
Into great saints.

O Bread of Life,
Food of Angels,
New Manna from Heaven,
Jesus Christ is given.

Leaning into Christ's chest,
I find my rest.

You Are Near

You are near,
I feel your heartbeat,
Streams of love pour forth,
Your steadiness is my comfort.

In this land of affliction,
Peace is our portion,
Peace in your Presence,
Partaking of the Eucharist.

Medicine of immortality,
Hope awakens,
Bread of Life,
Never leaves me forsaken.

Nourished by your Body,
Your nearness reaches to the depths of my soul,
All qualities that are yours,
Now infused into my innermost being.

You are near,
In this adoration chapel.
Under the appearance of bread,
You are here.

The Silent Faithful

he silent faithful,
    Adorers of your Eucharistic Presence,
    An army has arisen,
After your own likeness.

Though the Eucharist looks like simple bread,
And those who adore look lowly and meek,
We know that we behold Jesus,
And these adorers are counted strong when they are weak.

The silent faithful,
So humble and gentle,
Do not lose heart,
As you stare at our Lord.

You are being wise virgins,
The oil of intimacy is filling your cup.
Fill up your cups with silence, prayer, and the Eucharist,
This threefold intimacy is yours, whenever you get in front
    of the monstrance.

O silent faithful,
Do not lose faith,
Let your love burn bright,
As you stare into Jesus's face.

Bread of the Finest Wheat

Bread of the finest wheat,
Life-giving Bread.
Bread only in appearance,
The Holy One is present,
On his ground we tread,
Jesus is our daily Bread.

New Manna from Heaven,
Foreshadowed in Bethlehem,
House of Bread where Jesus lay,
The feeding trough of animals,
Our sweet Lord was placed.

Bread from Heaven now among us,
Living Flesh of Love,
God's gift now in us.
Bread of the finest wheat,
God himself within us,
So gentle, so sweet.

Unworthy Servants

nworthy servants,
We your People,
Unworthy servants,
Under every steeple.

We don't deserve a single thing,
Yet you give us yourself, O Lord,
This gift is everything.

Gift of Love,
Gift of Life,
Gift of Light,
Gift of Might.

Whatever you ask, we will do,
You are the Lord, Christ, Messiah,
Spotless Lamb and Judah's Lion.

Be it done unto us,
According to your word,
Only be with us,
Apart from you all things are absurd.

Withhold not yourself,

We always pray,

Give us this day, our daily Bread,

Your Eucharistic Presence,

Fulfills this request and fear is gone,

Death is dead.

Binding All Enemies

Binding all enemies,
The Bread of Life is Satan's bane,
Tearing from the Eucharist,
Is Satan's chief aim.

The Devil fears the Eucharist,
Source of communion,
The God-Man present, the Devil falls like lead,
Jesus crushes all schemes in the Serpent's head.

Devils and demons flee at the sight,
When a saint is filled with Eucharistic might.
Lucifer's light is shone to be dark,
When Light from Light is received,
The faithful are ignited,
Faith, hope, and love are sparked.

Enemies beware,
The Lord Jesus is near.
Flee from the Christ,
He puts an end to all your caused strife.

O Bread from Heaven,
Nourish your warriors,
Feed us this weapon,
Destroy these inferiors.

Tortured Glory

ortured glory,
Suffering Savior,
Mutilated for mankind,
Forgiveness on your lips.

Beaten to a pulp,
Blood pouring forth,
Offering all to your Father,
Suffering all for us.

Sacrifice so palpable and present,
In this Eucharistic Feast,
Beckoning the faithful to follow your path,
The path of the Cross, where we must meet.

Now suffering becomes a source of intimacy,
There is nothing to fear,
Death becomes a doorway to glory,
In glory you wipe away every tear.

O Eucharistic Presence of Jesus,
Both sacrifice and Resurrection,

Give us perseverance,
Through this participation.

Suffering and sacrifice,
Resurrection and new life,
The gift of yourself,
Brings glory for eternity and ends all strife.

Staring at Your Face

taring at your face,
I can feel your embrace.
I'm given all grace,
To run the race.
May sin leave no trace,
So, with pure heart, I can seek your face,
And cooperate so well with every dewdrop of grace.

Never Forsaken, Only Loved

ever forsaken, only loved,
Your constant Presence proves this love,
The love that perseveres and goes to the Cross.

O the Cross, the Cross,
Made present at every Mass.
Your Eucharistic Presence,
Embraces the totality of our life,
    suffering, and glory at last.

The Eucharist pulls the past into the present,
And future glory to the here and now.
Time collapses,
All angels and saints bow down in all the Masses.

O Eternal One,
Transcendent and real,
You come into my body,
Strengthening the Spirit's seal.

To you, O God, be glory forevermore.

Unveiled Veil

nveiled veil of Holy Mysteries,
Veil of separation torn,
Through the veiled Presence,
Of the God who was born.

First, you veiled your Divinity through
    your Sacred humanity,
Now, veiling both natures under the appearance of bread,
Faith pierces the veil
    and now we have Divine participation.

Though faith sees through the veil,
The longing for your Second Coming grows,
When, at last, our faith shall be sight,
And our direct experience of glory will overcome all night.

Face to face now in mystery,
Pushes us forward to eternity.
Hasten the day of your Return,
And thank you for your present Presence,
The Presence for which we all yearn.

Words Cannot Express

King Jesus,
   Words cannot express my love for you.
   I know you feel the same for me.
Perhaps this is why you speak in the silence,
And your silent Presence in this Eucharistic chapel is
Most simple, fitting, and altogether
   appropriate in expressing
Your love toward me.

Words cannot express your love for me,
Instead, you simply remain,
You simply be,
Be with your Beloved.

O Sacred Presence of Jesus,
   shrouded in mystery and silence,
You satisfy my soul, and keep me longing for more,
More of you.

Open the eyes of my heart,
For I want more of you,
Yet all of you is here,

And you promise you will never depart.

King Jesus,
Reigning in silence,
Reign in my heart,
All the days of my life.

A Father's Love

father's love expressed in this:
Giving his Son for the life of the world.

Jesus only did what he saw the Father do.
The Father pouring out his heart for mankind,
Jesus notices,
Sets his face like flint,
Expresses the Father's love through the Cross.
He came to seek and save the lost.

Even now, Jesus only does what he sees the Father doing.
The Father remaining with the Church,
Jesus notices,
Sets his face like flint,
Expresses the Father's love by becoming present
in the Sacred Host.
Jesus remains with his Church in the Eucharist by the
power of the Holy Ghost.

The Father still gives his one and only Son,
In every Mass you can partake of this priceless gift,
And receive the Father's love.

Blessed, Broke, Gave

Taking our bread into his hands,
Blessing the bread, eyes raised to Heaven,
Breaking the bread to share with the world,
Giving the bread to his disciples,
The crowds were fed with the multiplying bread.

Same liturgical action of Jesus later on in the Gospels
    at the Last Supper,
Revealing to all the meaning of this multiplication.

Taking our bread into his hands,
Blessing the bread, eyes raised to Heaven,
Breaking the bread, now become his Body,
Giving the Bread of Life to his disciples,
The crowds now nourished on the Body, Blood, Soul, and
    Divinity of Jesus Christ.

New Bread of the Presence,
New Manna,
New Lamb,
Bread become his Body,
Given through the Apostles to people in every land.

O sweet multiplication of loaves, so rich in foreshadowing
The age of the Church in all her journeying.
The Bread of Life given for all people,
Come, you nations of the earth, receive your King,
Under every Catholic Church steeple.

Choirs of Angels

Choirs of angels around your monstrance throne,
Silent singing, through ears of faith, I hear ringing.
Invisible spirits in obedience bow down,
Out of love, I join them and kneel to the ground.

Heaven is here as your Presence draws near,
Jubilation and joy surround, even in the silent sound.
Encountering God, so mystical, so mysterious,
Fulfilling my desires yet sparking me to be more desirous.

I am with you, yet I want to be with you more.
I am near you, yet I want to be closer still.
You hold nothing back, but give me your all,
Yet I can't help but want more of you, my all in all.

Unending praise resounds in the silence,
Choirs of angels raise their voices,
The saints join in the joy,
The best of all choices.

Joining the choirs of angels and saints,
I praise you, Jesus, and seek your face.

Perpetual Presence

 erpetual Presence,
God with us.
Never-ending source of life,
Presence of God within us, piercing hearts like a knife.

O Sacrament Divine,
Deserving of all my love.
Greatest gift given,
Given from above.

Perpetual Presence,
O Eucharistic God.
The Risen One among us,
We bring you joyful laud.

All for the Sacred and Eucharistic Heart of Jesus

 ll for the Sacred and Eucharistic Heart of Jesus,
Heart so full of love, faithfulness, and goodness.
Sacrificial love,
A love that remains,
Death could not defeat,
The Risen Lord takes his Heavenly Seat.

All through the Sorrowful
   and Immaculate Heart of Mary,
Heart so tender and reflective of the Light.
Pondering God's Presence,
Mary points us towards her Son,
   the Sun of Justice and Might.
The path marked out leads to the Cross,
Help us, Mary, to go with Jesus to the end,
For if we persevere, we will reign with Jesus,
The Lord to whom every knee will bend.

All in union with St. Joseph,
The Guardian of Jesus and Mary,

Original adorer of God
   within the tabernacle of Mary's body.
Holding Jesus, gazing at God's face,
Help us, St. Joseph, to be like you,
To adore Jesus and cooperate with God's grace.

All for the Sacred and Eucharistic Heart of Jesus,
All through the Sorrowful and Immaculate Heart of Mary,
All in union with St. Joseph.
Amen.

Euchoetry.com

Become part of the movement!

Being in the Presence of the Creator often unleashes our own creativity. You are invited to spend time in Eucharistic Adoration*, write a poem, and submit that poem on euchoetry.com.

The long-term vision of euchoetry.com is to compile these poems into books so that people can bring a hard copy of these poems into Adoration with them and be ignited in their faith and filled with awe and wonder as they worship Jesus Christ in the Eucharist. This book is the first installment featuring the poems of Eric Robinson, but the subsequent books that will hopefully come could include your own poems written in God's Presence!

Be transfigured in Adoration, write a poem, and transform the world.

*While the poems in this volume were all first handwritten in Eucharistic Adoration with the Blessed Sacrament exposed in a monstrance, you are also encouraged to submit poems to euchoetry.com that you have written while adoring Jesus hidden in the tabernacle of a Catholic Church.

About the Author

Eric Robinson is a Catholic husband, father, and evangelist on mission to draw all people into full communion with the Holy Catholic Church and to set everyone on fire with the Gospel of Jesus Christ through prayer, teaching, works of mercy, and family life. To fulfill the teaching component of this mission, he has written five books: *Thoughts of a Changed Mind: Letters from Father to Son* (2016), *Thoughts of a Sacramental Mind* (2020), *Visible Unity: A Calling of Christ for the Church* (2020), *Essays in the Deep: Faith & Reason, Meaning & Morality, Protestantism & Catholic Thought* (2021), and this book, *Euchoetry: Poems in the Presence* (2023). He also started a YouTube channel, website, and podcast under the name, "Polycarp's Paradigm."

Eric was not always a Catholic. In fact, he grew up without the Eucharist as an Evangelical Protestant in various denominations, but his hunger for the truth and his desire to be part of the early Church eventually led him into the Catholic Church in 2015. Since that time, Eric has come to love our Lord in the Eucharist and has had the privilege of taking Holy Communion to the sick and homebound, which has been his favorite ministry up to this point. Additionally, he has taught classes for Adult and Youth Faith Formation and has his Master of Arts in Theology from Holy Apostles College & Seminary.

Eric is very excited about euchoetry.com so he can have the chance to read beautiful poems by other people and be inspired by their love for the Lord in the Eucharist.

Made in the USA
Middletown, DE
20 April 2023

29147007R00094